A History of Hip-Hop: The Roots of
Rap
Thomas Hatch
AR B.L.: 3.6
Points: 0.5   MG

A History of Hip-Hop

The Roots of Rap

by Thomas Hatch

Reading Consultant:
Timothy Rasinski, Ph.D.
Professor of Reading Education
Kent State University

Content Consultant:
Dr. Will Patterson
Assistant Director
African American Studies Research Program
University of Illinois at Champaign Urbana

Red Brick™ Learning

Published by Red Brick™ Learning
7825 Telegraph Road, Bloomington, Minnesota 55438
http://www.redbricklearning.com

Library of Congress Cataloging-in-Publication Data
Hatch, Thomas, 1947–
   A history of hip-hop: the roots of rap / by Thomas Hatch.
   p. cm.—(High five reading)
   Includes bibliographical references and index.
   ISBN 0-7368-5750-8 (soft cover)—ISBN 0-7368-5740-0 (hard cover)
   1. Rap (Music)—History and criticism—Juvenile literature.
   2. Hip-hop—United States—Juvenile literature. I. Title. II. Series.
ML3531.H38 2006
782.421649'09—dc22
                   2005011137

Created by Kent Publishing Services, Inc.
Designed by Signature Design Group, Inc.
Edited by Jerry Ruff, Managing Editor, Red Brick™ Learning
Red Brick™ Learning Editorial Director: Mary Lindeen

This publisher has made every effort to trace ownership of all copyrighted
material and to secure necessary permissions. In the event of any questions
arising as to the use of any material, the publisher, while expressing regret for
any inadvertent error, will be happy to make necessary corrections.

Photo Credits:
Cover, pages 24, 35, RM1/Wenn Photos; page 4, Henry Ditz/Corbis; pages 6,
12, Associated Press, A/P; page 8, Douglas Kirkland, Corbis; page 15, Scott
Gries, Getty Images; page 16, Bettmann/Corbis; page 18, Dan Regan, Getty
Images; page 20, Helena Kubicka, Zarchive/Zuma Press; page 22, Carl Juste,
KRT Photos; page 26, Richard B. Levine, Photographers Showcase; page 28,
Juerg Mueller, EPA Photos; page 30, Associated Press A/P; page 33, Victoria
Chandler, Avantis/Zuma Press; page 36, Mariana Bazo, Reuters Photo Archive;
page 38, Matthew Cavanaugh, Getty Images; page 40, STR/EPA Photos; page
43, Dara Kushner/INFGoff.com/Photographers Showcase

Printed in the United States of America.

1 2 3 4 5 6 11 10 09 08 07 06 05

Table of Contents

Jimi Hendrix was a rock star in the 1960s.

CHAPTER 1

1970: The Beat Changes

The Beatles. Jimi Hendrix. The Doors. The Who. Do you know those names? They are all rock stars from the 1960s. But music is always changing. What music do you and your friends listen to today? Will you listen to the same music tomorrow?

Don't Worry

Imagine the year is 1970. You turn on the radio. The number-one song is playing, "Raindrops Keep Falling on My Head." The sound is easygoing. The words tell people not to worry, everything is okay.

The South Bronx

But everything is not okay. Your own home is in a tough place. You live in the South Bronx, New York. Your street is dangerous. You have to be careful of the **gangs**.

Graffiti on a subway train

---

gang (GANG): an organized group of people who spend a great deal of time together

Graffiti

You look out the window. A train is passing. The train tracks are high up off the street. **Graffiti** covers the train cars. Kids, mostly, did this colorful writing.

In fact, graffiti writing is a kind of contest. Kids make up names for themselves. These names are called *tags*. The kids write their tags all over town. Some writers are famous. Their tags seem to be everywhere.

Some graffiti writers join small groups of writers called *crews*. These crews sometimes use spray paint. They make huge, colorful letters. Crews write at night so they don't get caught. Graffiti writing is illegal.

---

graffiti (gruh-FEE-tee): pictures or words drawn on walls, subway cars, or other surfaces

Disco Is Hot

On your way to school, disco music plays on your radio. Disco is popular now, too. Disco has a stronger beat. But still it doesn't seem like music about your life.

One time you peeked into a disco club. The dance crowd was dressed real **slick**. Everyone looked rich. The men wore gold chains. The women wore dresses and high heels.

John Travolta played a disco dancer in the movie Saturday Night Fever.

slick (SLIK): fancy; with style

DJs and MCs

Pete DJ Jones is the best disco **DJ** around. He has his own **sound system**. He knows how to make one song blend into the next. That way, the music and beat never stop. This keeps a crowd dancing.

Jones works with an **MC** named JT Hollywood. JT talks to the crowd at parties. He is the host. The host and DJ work together to keep everyone dancing.

DJ (DEE-jay): short for *disc jockey*; a person who plays records for dancing at parties
sound system (SOUND SISS-tuhm): equipment for playing records
MC (em-SEE): short for *master of ceremonies*; a person who hosts an event

Meet Herc

At school, you spot your friend Herc. Herc's real name is Clive Campbell. Clive likes to work out. Everyone calls him Herc, for **Hercules**. He's from Jamaica (juh-MAY-kuh). Herc moved to the South Bronx three years ago. He's into music.

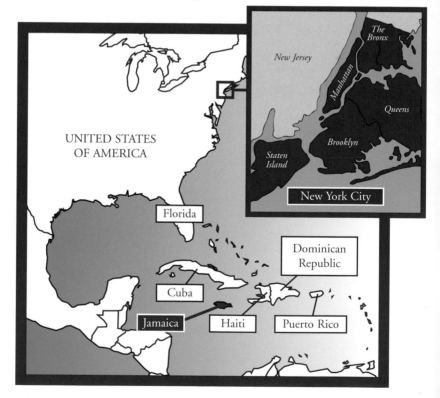

Hercules (HUR-kyoo-leez): a hero from Greek and Roman myths who was very strong and powerful

Neighborhoods Change

Your neighborhood in the South Bronx is changing. Many people want a safer place to live. Some are moving out.

Rent in the South Bronx is cheap. More people from Jamaica move there. They don't have much money. But they want a better life.

Rhythm and Words

The Jamaicans bring their music with them. The music is called *reggae* (RAY-gay). Reggae has a catchy **rhythm** that you like. The words are important, too. They don't just make you feel good. They tell about real life.

Herc begins to learn about reggae. In a few years, he will be the most famous DJ in New York. What do you think his music will be like?

---

rhythm (RITH-uhm): a regular beat in music, poetry, or dance

*Teens made their own music in the poor
South Bronx neighborhood in New York.*

CHAPTER 2

1974: Herc Spins the Break-beat

Herc and other South Bronx teenagers were poor.
They couldn't go to clubs to listen to DJs.
Instead, they made their own music.

Making Music

In Jamaica, people held dances outside or in dancehalls. DJs set up sound systems and played records. By 1974, there were dances like these in the South Bronx.

People in the South Bronx would put a record on a **turntable**. Then they would drop the needle at the spot on the record with the best dance music.

---

turntable (TURN-tay-buhl): a round surface that spins and is used in playing phonograph records

Herc's New Name

Herc built his own sound system. He had two turntables. He also changed his name to DJ Kool Herc.

Looking for Something New

Herc loved to **entertain**. He would switch from song to song. He acted as MC, too. Herc would talk while the music played. "Shake it, shake it," he would say to keep the crowd dancing.

Herc was always looking for new ways to keep people dancing. What do you think he tried next?

---

entertain (en-tur-TAYN): to amuse and interest someone

DJ Kool Herc

Tina Turner and James Brown were popular stars who sang and danced to funk music.

A New Beat

Herc's fans liked **funk** music the best.
Herc liked funk, too. He liked the breaks
between the **lyrics**. In these breaks, the
music kept going strong.

Herc liked to mix these breaks. To do this,
he used two copies of the same record on two
turntables. First he would play a break from
one record. Then he would play the same
break from the other record. He did this over
and over to keep the beat going. Herc called
this style of music a *break-beat*.

People loved it. Later this style would be
called *dubbing* or *remixing*.

---

funk (FUHNGK): a type of music with a heavy beat
lyric (LIHR-ik): the words to a song

Mixing the Beat

DJ Kool Herc would also MC as he played. He would make rhymes. His words added to the beat. In Jamaica, using words like this is called *toasting*. What Herc was doing would later be called *rapping*.

Others copied Herc. DJs began to make their own songs. They took pieces of music from records and put them together in new ways. They spoke their rhymes over the break-beat. They became rappers.

Breakdancing

Gangs also came to hear Herc and to dance. Gang members soon found a new way to battle each other. They began to compete to see which gang could dance better!

The dancers invented fancy moves. Some were style moves with fancy footwork. Others were power moves. For these, the dancer would drop to the floor and kick out or spin on his head.

The dancers formed crews. These groups of friends would dance together. The crews danced during the break-beats. They tried new moves to show off to the crowd.

This breakdancer is doing a power move.

Music, Dance, and Art
Come Together

The Bronx kids loved DJ Kool Herc's style. These kids didn't dress slick like the disco crowd. The boys didn't wear gold chains. The girls didn't wear fancy dresses and heels. These kids wore regular street clothes.

Herc's fans loved **DJing** and rapping. They loved breakdancing and graffiti. They became the B-Boys and B-Girls— the break boys, the Bronx boys, the beat boys, the beat girls.

Hip-Hop culture was born. It spread fast. But what was it really all about?

A rapper performs live.

DJing (DEE-jay-ing): disc jockeying; playing music like a disc jockey

*The Hip-Hop culture is shown
in the graffiti on these walls.*

CHAPTER 3

1974 to 1978: Hip-Hop Culture Spreads

*A culture is the special **customs**, skills, and art of a group of people. What is Hip-Hop culture then?*

Hip-Hop Culture

Hip-Hop is a culture. One reason is that Hip-Hop is about making art. Hip-Hop art includes music, poetry, dance, and painting.

Hip-Hop isn't just about art, though. Hip-Hop also is a way to live your life. Who helped Hip-Hop change and grow?

---

custom (KUHSS-tuhm): something people do regularly

Punch-Phasing

Many DJs learned from DJ Kool Herc. Grandmaster Flash was one of them. His real name is Joseph Saddler. Flash learned how to cut between records from Herc.

Flash also had his own style. He began to take part of one record and play it at the same time as another. This is called *mixing*. Flash also added loud, popping sounds to music. He called this *punch-phasing*.

Grandmaster Flash invented mixing.

Scratching

Theodore Livingston invented scratching. To do this, he would place his fingertip on a spinning record to stop it. Then he would move the record back and forth to make a scratchy sound.

Livingston was 13 years old when he invented scratching. Later, he became a DJ known as Grand Wizard Theodore. Today, DJs around the world use scratching.

A DJ is scratching this record.

Afrika Bambaataa

Another South Bronx teenager also learned to DJ in the 1970s. His name was Kevin Donovan. He changed his name to Afrika Bambaataa (bam-BAH-tah). This name means "**affectionate** leader." People called him Bam.

affectionate (uh-FEK-shuh-nuht): loving

Universal Zulu Nation

Bam started his own club. His club gave gang members a way to quit the gangs. Bam named his club Universal Zulu Nation. The club helped get rid of drug dealers. They helped people in need. They looked out for older people. Hip-Hop culture was important to everyone in the club.

In this way, Bam helped young people build pride and **self-confidence.** He helped them learn new things. They began to look at their lives in a different way.

A Zulu Nation member shows off his jacket.

self-confidence (SELF KON-fuh-denss): being sure of your own abilities and worth

Members of Kraftwerk perform.
Kraftwerk *means "power plant."*

Electro Funk

Bam liked music. He put together a sound system and became a DJ. Bam played at parties around New York City. He was one of the first to use machines that made drum and computer sounds to add to his music.

Bam listened to Kraftwerk. This German group made unusual music. Sometimes the music sounded like factory noise. Other times it sounded like zapping **electricity** or **tribal** drums. Bam loved Kraftwerk's sound. Bam used this music to make his own.

Hip-Hop Spreads

By 1978, Hip-Hop culture had spread through the Bronx. It spread through the rest of New York City as well. How did it become popular around the world?

---

electricity (i-lek-TRISS-uh-tee): a form of energy
tribal (TRYE-buhl): having to do with people who share the same ancestors, customs, and laws

Hip-Hop continued to grow in the early 1980s.

CHAPTER 4

1978 to 1984: Hip-Hop Nation

By 1978, Herc, Flash, and Bam were the top DJs in New York. They had their own house parties and block parties. But soon, Hip-Hop began to change.

Rappers

As time went on, MCs became rappers. They got their **props** from **boasting**. They **taunted** each other. DJs, rappers, and B-Boys teamed up to see who could rap the best.

New rap groups formed. A record company was started just for rap artists. It was called Sugar Hill Records.

---

props (PROPS): praise and recognition
boast (BOHST): to brag
taunt (TAWNT): to tease

Rapper's Delight

The first hit rap song was "Rapper's Delight," by the Sugar Hill Gang. Big Bank Hank, Henry Jackson, was the rapper. The song came out in 1979. Here are some of the words.

Rapper's Delight

i said a hip hop the hippie the hippie
to the hip hip hop, you don't stop
the rock it to the bang bang boogie say up jumped the boogie
to the rhythm of the boogie, the beat

now what you hear is not a test—i'm rappin to the beat
and me, the groove, and my friends are gonna try to
*   move your feet*
see i am wonder mike and i like to say hello
to the black, to the white, the red, and the brown, the
*   purple and yellow*

Sugar Hill Gang

33

The Furious Five

Grandmaster Flash joined a rap group. They called themselves the Furious Five. Their song "The Message" came out in 1982. It sold more than 1 million copies. "The Message" was more than just party music. It talked about **social** problems.

Around the World

Also in 1982, Afrika Bambaataa was part of the first Hip-Hop tour to go to Europe. Hip-Hop had become a big business. People knew about it around the world.

Rap is a big part of Hip-Hop. But the roots of rap go much deeper. Where do you think rap really begins?

---

social (SOH-shuhl): having to do with the way people live together

The Message

Can't take the smell—can't take the noise
Got no money to move out
I guess I got no choice
Rats in the front room, roaches in the back
Junkie's in the alley with a baseball bat
I tried to get away, but I couldn't get far
'Cause the man with the tow truck repossessed my car
Don't push me, 'cause I'm close to the edge
I'm trying not to lose my head
It's like a jungle sometimes, it makes me wonder how
I keep from going under

Grandmaster Flash performs.

This Brazilian dancer shows how capoeira is played.

— CHAPTER **5** —

The Roots of Rap

Hip-Hop culture came from ghetto life in the Bronx.
But the ideas behind Hip-Hop go far back in history.

Hip-Hop and History

Many things in Hip-Hop aren't really new.
Long ago, Egyptians (ee-JIP-shuhns) wrote
their names on the walls of the pyramids.
The graffiti writers were doing the same
with their tags.

In Africa, warriors once danced to show
skill and strength. In Brazil, players make
a circle to play capoeira (KAP-oh-AY-ruh).
As music is played, the players do handstands
and backflips to show their power. Both
these **traditions** look like breakdancing.

---

tradition (truh-DISH-uhn): a custom, belief, or idea that
is handed down from one generation to the next

A woman calls out during a church service.

Playing the Dozens

Many things in African American culture also led to rap. Playing the Dozens is an African American game. Players taunt each other to win respect. They say things like, *"You're so slow it takes you an hour to cook MINUTE® rice."* The taunts can be funny. But they can be mean, too.

Rappers also tease and taunt each other. At DJ and MC battles, rappers use words to battle for respect.

The African American Church

Preachers also mix music and talk. One preaching style is call-and-response. The preacher speaks to a beat or with a strong rhythm. The crowd calls or talks back. MCs use this style, too.

The Griot

In West Africa, a griot (GREE-oh) is a storyteller. *Griot* means "news singer." The griot keeps the people's history and teaches it to others.

The MC is like a griot. MCs tell stories of people's lives.

Kasse Mady Diabaté is one of Mali's best known "griot" singers.

Not Just Men

In Hip-Hop, women can be MCs, too. Salt-N-Pepa and Queen Latifah are Hip-Hop stars today. Their songs tell stories about life. These women sing, rap, and entertain.

Deep in History

In the 1970s, a new culture was born. It came to be called Hip-Hop. This culture started in the Bronx. But it had roots from many countries and cultures around the world.

Today, Hip-Hop and rap are bigger than ever. We hear rap music on the radio, TV, and in movies. Today's DJs and MCs learned from Herc, Flash, and Bam. Others will now learn from them. That is how history works!

Epilogue

Hip-Hop culture was born in 1974.
By 1984, it was big business. That year,
Hip-Hop became **mainstream**. Two people
who helped make Hip-Hop popular were
Joseph and Russell Simmons.

Run DMC

Run (Joseph Simmons) was a DJ. Jam
Master Jay (Jason Mizell) was a DJ, too.
D (Darryl McDaniels) was an MC.
Together they put out *RUN DMC* in 1984.
This was the first rap **album** ever made.

---

mainstream (MAYN-streem): a trend or style that most
people have heard of
album (AL-buhm): a collection of music recorded on a
record, tape, or CD

42

Russell Simmons

Russell Simmons is Joseph's older brother. Russell started Def Jam Records. He also made a movie about Hip-Hop called *Krush Groove*. Russell started Phat Farm Clothes. He even made the movie *The Nutty Professor*, starring Eddie Murphy.

Russell Simmons

Glossary

affectionate (uh-FEK-shuh-nuht): loving

album (AL-buhm): a collection of music recorded on a record, tape, or CD

boast (BOHST): to brag

custom (KUHSS-tuhm): something people do regularly

DJ (DEE-jay): short for *disc jockey*; a person who plays records for dancing at parties

DJing (DEE-jay-ing): disc jockeying; playing music like a disc jockey

electricity (i-lek-TRISS-uh-tee): a form of energy

entertain (en-tur-TAYN): to amuse and interest someone

funk (FUHNGK): a type of music with a heavy beat

gang (GANG): an organized group of people who spend a great deal of time together

graffiti (gruh-FEE-tee): pictures or words drawn on walls, subway cars, or other surfaces

Hercules (HUR-kyoo-leez): a hero from Greek and Roman myths who was very strong and powerful

lyric (LIHR-ik): the words to a song

mainstream (MAYN-streem): a trend or style that most people have heard of

44

MC (em-SEE): short for *master of ceremonies*; a person who hosts an event

props (PROPS): praise and recognition

rhythm (RITH-uhm): a regular beat in music, poetry, or dance

self-confidence (SELF KON-fuh-denss): being sure of your own abilities and worth

slick (SLIK): fancy; with style

social (SOH-shuhl): having to do with the way people live together

sound system (SOUND SISS-tuhm): equipment for playing records

taunt (TAWNT): to tease

tradition (truh-DISH-uhn): a custom, belief, or idea that is handed down from one generation to the next

tribal (TRYE-buhl): having to do with people who share the same ancestors, customs, and laws

turntable (TURN-tay-buhl): a round surface that spins and is used in playing phonograph records

Bibliography

Bankston, John. *Alicia Keys: Hip-Hop Superstars.* Blue Banner Biographies. Hockessin, Del.: Mitchell Lane Publishers, 2004.

Bankston, John. *Jay-Z: Hip-Hop Superstars.* Blue Banner Biographies. Hockessin, Del.: Mitchell Lane Publishers, 2004.

Bankston, John. *Missy Elliot: Hip-Hop Superstars.* Blue Banner Biographies. Hockessin, Del.: Mitchell Lane Publishers, 2004.

Haskins, James. *One Nation Under Groove: Rap Music and Its Roots.* New York: Hyperion, 2000.

Lommel, Cookie. *The History of Rap Music.* African American Achievers. Philadelphia: Chelsea House, 2001.

Morreale, Marie. *Pop People: Lil' Romeo.* New York: Scholastic, 2004.

Useful Addresses

Rock and Roll Hall of Fame and Museum
One Key Plaza
751 Erieside Avenue
Cleveland, OH 44114

Stax Museum of American Soul Music
926 E. McLemore Avenue
Memphis, TN 38106

Internet Sites

Davy D's Hip Hop Daily News
http://www.daveyd.com

Rap/Hip-Hop
http://www.rap.about.com

rapworld
http://www.rapworld.com/history

Index